PEACOCK HOUSE

CHICKEN HOUSE

CHAPEL

BARN

ANTONIA'S HOUSE

WELL HOUSE

GATEHOUSE

ONE MAN'S FOLLY

THE EXCEPTIONAL HOUSES
OF FURLOW GATEWOOD

ONE MAN'S FOLLY

THE EXCEPTIONAL HOUSES OF FURLOW GATEWOOD

Julia Reed

Foreword and Afterword by Bunny Williams

Photography by Rodney Collins and Paul Costello

RIZZOLI
NEW YORK

New York · Paris · London · Milan

To John Rosselli and Bunny Williams,
without whom this book
would have never happened.
— *Furlow Gatewood*

TABLE OF CONTENTS

FOREWORD

Furlow Gatewood is one of the most talented and influential members of America's design community—and one that you have likely never heard of. A dear friend and constant inspiration, he has created an amazing compound of houses on his family's property in Georgia, but has always chosen to maintain a low profile—until now. At the urging of his many admirers in the trade, he has finally agreed to open the doors to his creations so that others can see what we have all long known. Furlow is possessed of boundless style, a fearless talent, and a singular eye. Howard Christian, the design editor of *Architectural Digest* (and another of Furlow's close friends), puts it best:

Better than anyone I know, Furlow represents to me a person whose identity is so completely in tune with what he believes in, what interests him. Most of us compromise. Not so Furlow. His love of beauty and scale is the engine of his life; it guides and informs everything he does. When you hear Furlow utter the phrase "good-looking" in his lovely seasoned accent, you know that you need to open your eyes and pay attention. He is ahead of you.

This book is a journey through the four magical houses that Furlow has created on his family enclave in Americus, Georgia, each of which is chock-full of the treasures he has amassed in more than sixty years of avid collecting. They include the renovated carriage house original to the property, a house he designed and built from scratch, and two period nineteenth-century houses that he moved onto the land from nearby towns. The complex was created for no other reason than to indulge Furlow's passion for architecture, design, and collecting. The end result is nothing less than one of the most unique arrays of domestic architecture in America. Unlike Henry Francis du Pont, who created the Winterthur Museum, Furlow has not had limitless funds. And unlike Henry Sleeper, who built Beauport in Gloucester, Massachusetts, partly as a showcase for his design business, he has never been motivated by commercial reasons. But the factors that

really set Furlow's houses apart from any others I've seen are his innate taste and flair, his creative use of architectural elements, his flawless eye for decoration, and his seemingly offhand knack for putting together sublime objects—some good, some merely decorative—to create the most special, comfortable interiors I have ever had the good fortune to visit.

Furlow was born in 1921 in Americus, Georgia, a wealthy farm town. Beautiful pecan groves and fields of peanuts and cotton surround this county seat. His family has lived here for four generations. From an early age he had the collecting bug. His first purchase was a pair of blue milk glass tureens (a hen and a rooster) he bought with money from his paper route. Furlow joined the army at the beginning of the Second World War, and at the end of 1944 he returned to Americus to open Gatewood's Flowers, where he also began selling some antiques. After a few years, he attended design school in New York City but soon realized his passion was for antiques. Too bad, as he would have made a great interior designer. Furlow then opened a small antiques shop near Second Avenue in the sixties; at that time Second Avenue was the home to many wonderful eccentric antiques shops; John Rosselli (now my husband) was the owner of another small shop nearby. In the early sixties, John suggested that his friend Furlow combine their inventory into one operation, an arrangement that would allow John to travel abroad on extended shopping sprees while Furlow ran the antiques store. This was the beginning of the collaboration, which continues today, that has made John Rosselli International the must-go-to source for all designers. In my early twenties, when I was an employee of the firm Parish-Hadley, Mrs. Parish suggested that I go to the shop, where she knew I would find everything we needed for a particular project. It was there that I met John and Furlow. Furlow was movie-star handsome with sparkling eyes and the softest, sexiest Southern accent ever. To this day all my friends of every age are just mad about Furlow. Miles Redd describes him beautifully:

Had I not had the good fortune of working for antiques maestro John Rosselli, I may never have met this remarkable, incredibly inspiring man. Working in John's repository of chic-ness was my first job after college. Thrilled to be starting "real" life, I reported to my first day of duty in a look more suited to Gatsby on the golf course than humble shopkeeper. But I was young and filled with the fantasy of possibility, and Furlow, being a romantic, kindly indulged me. Since I was the new kid, one of the other longtime employees handed me a can of Easy-Off and some filthy andirons and, with a dismissive glance, ordered me to clean them on the street. Maid service in immaculate cream flannel trousers, I would soon learn, is the reality of decorating. Illusion dashed, I was given comfort and support by Furlow, who every morning greeted us with the warmest "Good morning" and a cup of tea (with lots of cream and sugar).

Previous page: Young Furlow in a Cord convertible. Opposite, clockwise from top left: Furlow with his good friend and contractor Jimmy Fuller; John Rosselli with Phillip, one of Furlow's two Italian greyhounds, in the Barn; decorative painter Bob Christian begins work on the floor in the Lumpkin House; and Julia Reed talks with carpenter Joe McElroy.

During the 1950s and sixties Furlow spent a lot of time in Americus visiting his mother. It was then that he began restoring the carriage house, which was next to his childhood home where his mother still lived. Little by little, over many years, bedrooms were added, the Gothic lattice dining room was created, the kitchen expanded. Sometimes a room would be constructed to incorporate pieces of furniture Furlow had to have. Martha McLanahand, a dear friend, tells the story of arriving in the Barn and finding a huge chinoiserie daybed with no mattress in the entrance hall. This was because there was no room for it, but that never deterred Furlow. He simply built a divine dressing room and bath onto a beautiful back bedroom and placed the daybed in the middle of the space. Years later, I was with Furlow when he spotted the most magnificent eighteenth-century Italian painted armoire at a pier show from the dealer Kenny Ball. He had to have it. It was ten feet tall (huge scale is a Furlow trademark), and this became the closet for the dressing room.

Finding a particular treasure (or set of them) has often been the trigger for Furlow's creativity. Little did I ever expect that twenty pieces of unusual lattice panels, which he bought in Connecticut one weekend while we were shopping at the dealer Michael Trapp's, would become the back porch of what is now known as the Peacock House.

Furlow is completely self-educated. He never attended architecture school but he has taken a tour of every great nineteenth-century house in Georgia. His hours of devouring *Country Life* magazine and countless books on architecture and furniture have helped him develop an amazing eye. He would rather read *Antiques* magazine than *Vanity Fair*. The other amazing part of the story of Furlow and his houses is his relationship with Jimmy Fuller, his friend and contractor, and Joe McElroy, a master carpenter and craftsman. The work on the buildings and the details of the interior restoration were done with no elaborate architectural drawings, often with just Furlow's vision and a picture from a book or magazine. In each structure, character was immediately created by the use of found objects, old paneling, fabulous period mantels, or unique old windows. Period door surrounds were incorporated into many rooms, giving the spaces the sense that they have always been there.

Gil Schafer, the great American architect, made this comment after a trip to Americus:

When you're there among his collections, you learn quickly to look at things in a new way. The play of scale, the mix of intimate and grand, fancy and humble, show you that these juxtapositions can enliven the character of everything—architecture, furniture, fabric, and objects. Ultimately, you are enveloped by the same feeling of delight that has permeated all that Furlow has done there for the past sixty years.

One of the greatest joys of my life has been the thousands of miles I have traveled with John and Furlow on the hunt for treasures for our various shops and homes. Almost every weekend was spent at an antiques fair or going from shop to shop in Georgia, Connecticut, Maine, and New York. Vacations were trips to France, India, Morocco, England, always on a quest for unique objects. I can still see Furlow in the market in Jaipur, India (a place we love), sitting on a stack of textiles, with a young boy running up and down the market trying to please Furlow, who was on a hunt for red-and-white blocked cottons to cover the furniture on the porch in the Barn. The boy was so good that Furlow wanted to bring him back to work as a salesperson in the shop. That didn't happen, but five new duffel bags had to be purchased to ship our finds home.

To fully appreciate Furlow, you have to understand that this man loves animals more than anyone I know. He has never had less than four dogs, a cat or two, and, more recently, dozens of peacocks. The several breeds of dogs he's owned include beautiful whippets, Italian greyhounds, and Azawakhs, and there is always space in Furlow's house for the stray that no one wants or can take care of anymore. On a trip to France, John and I found a fabulous book, *Les Chiens*, which we knew Furlow would love. Little did we imagine that he would be moonstruck by an Azawakh (an African sight hound we had never heard of) from a picture and decided he had to have one. After many, many calls to France by my dear assistant, May Daouk, who is fluent in French, a female Azawakh was purchased and sent on her way to America and the waiting arms of a besotted Furlow. Cordelia turned out to be a crazy dog. She bonded with Furlow and no one else. Though she was quite mad, I think she was one of Furlow's favorite dogs ever. Once, when we were in India waiting in the early morning hours for the sun to rise over the Taj Mahal, Furlow and I discovered a tiny puppy. We then spent the next couple of hours trying to figure out how to get the puppy, whom we named Taj, back to America. The sun finally brought into view not only the exquisite Taj Mahal but also the sight of the mother and her other puppies, which for Furlow and me was even more special.

Furlow is a very private person, a perfect Southern gentleman with the most beautiful manners. The essence of this man is his care and consideration for others. He never arrives without his delicious homemade cheese straws, a bag of pecans, pounds of the best bacon ever, and a caramel cake. He has a real sweet tooth. He also has an effortless way of making everyone feel so special. When you are his guest, he puts you thoroughly at ease. If you would like to meet Furlow, you can find him having lunch at Granny's Kitchen every day in Americus, or, on the third Thursday of each month, at Scott's Antiques Market in Atlanta. At ninety-two, he is still on the hunt.

—Bunny Williams

INTRODUCTION

Ifirst met Furlow Gatewood when I (along with my dog Henry) was invited by Bunny Williams and John Rosselli to join them for a long weekend at his compound in Americus, Georgia. Expected for dinner, I arrived at well past ten—his rather exotic address, Peacock Alley, had not turned up anywhere on my iPhone's GPS and I'd stupidly forgotten about the hour-later time difference. Each time I called with updates on my latest wrong turn, I begged the group to have dinner without me, to go to bed, to let me slip into the Barn (Furlow's main residence and where we were all ensconced) unannounced. But Furlow would have none of it. When I finally got close to the all-but-hidden drive, there he was in the middle of the pitch-black road, waving me in with a flashlight.

Embarrassed, in need of a drink, and with an equally hungry/thirsty beagle in tow, I was immediately made at home by the three of them. Henry was fed, the plate of Furlow's famous cheese straws replenished, a stiff Scotch produced. It was close to midnight before we finally sat down to dinner, but such is Furlow's innate courtliness and refinement that I was made to feel as though that were his usual routine.

Over the next few days, I became a privileged citizen of Furlow's enchanted universe. Located about five minutes from the Ruby Tuesday where I'd unsuccessfully sought directions, it could easily be on a different planet—one where things of only the utmost beauty or interest or soul are allowed, whether they be object (blue-and-white Chinese porcelain, exquisite eighteenth-century doors and mantels), flora (an allée of potted Nikko Blue hydrangeas, citrus trees, and fragrant gardenias), or fauna (more than forty stunning peacocks, two Italian greyhounds named Phillip and Will, two African Azawakhs named Hawkins and Cleon, a black-and-white cat christened Kitty, and a yellow cat named Cat).

During the entire trip, I never once turned on my computer (no wireless), rarely used my cell phone (bad service), and never once looked at the television (though there were a couple of prehistoric ones around). Instead, we talked and cooked, walked the grounds and ogled the houses, and played with the dogs and mixed up cocktails (though not necessarily in that order). It was the only time in Henry's hound-dog life that he didn't try to escape through any barely opened door. Instead, when he was accidentally let out, he waited patiently to be allowed back in. Who could blame him?

When I awoke on that first morning, I was scarcely prepared for what I saw—and what you are about to discover on these pages. As artist and decorative painter Bob Christian says about the Barn, the place is a "visual feast." But it's hardly the only one. The grounds hold one architectural surprise after another: the Peacock House, the Cuthbert House, the Lumpkin House, and a succession of jewel-box-like outbuildings. The most astonishing thing of all is that with the exception of the Barn, the whole compound has been assembled and landscaped within the last ten years, while Furlow was in his eighties.

It also was done without any clear plan. Says Joe McElroy, a master carpenter who has worked on many of Furlow's "follies": "He'll just set something down and say, 'Joe, do you think you could build me a house around this?'" As it happens, "this" is invariably some fabulous window or door—the kind of architectural fragment that Furlow says he started buying up decades ago, long before "other people caught on to how valuable they are."

As Bunny says in her foreword, Furlow began collecting when he was just a child of eight or nine, when he bought a pair of milk glass chickens from his great-aunt Nanie Lou, his grandmother Gatewood's sister, with money from his paper route. "She had everything growing up," he says. "But then when the Depression came they lost it all. She and her husband moved to a small farm in the country with an outhouse, but she never complained. She just opened a little antiques shop in the barn on the place and I'd get on my bicycle and ride the three miles over there to see her."

Furlow's family has deep roots in Georgia. His maternal great-grandfather was the president of the Savannah, Americus & Montgomery Railroad, which ran from Savannah to a little town called Cordele, named after his daughter Cordelia, Furlow's grandmother and the namesake of his first Azawakh. His childhood, he says, was idyllic, with freedom to roam and lots of visits to the big Victorian house belonging to his grandmother, who would protect him when he played hooky from school.

Furlow was raised with his two late siblings, sister Flora and an athletic brother, nicknamed "Chick." Though their mother, Flora, lived to be ninety-three, their father, Furlow (also known as "Big Gator"), died while still in his fifties. Furlow reports that his mother was "interested in nice things, but she didn't have a lot of money." To make ends meet after her husband's death, Flora would occasionally sell off an acre or two of the farm, the remnants of which Furlow lives on now, in close proximity to a niece and a nephew.

Furlow didn't make the move to Manhattan until he was in his thirties, after a stint in the air force (served in the Panhandle of Texas, which he loathed) and a few years as the proprietor of a flower shop, which he found only marginally more fulfilling. "In those days, I liked to have fun, and when all my friends were celebrating during holidays, that's when I'd have to go to work."

In New York, he met John Rosselli, who would become his closest friend and partner in an antiques business, and found his calling. Bob Christian, a fellow Georgian whose family and Furlow's go way back, got a job at the legendary shop when he was an aspiring artist just out of college. He describes a riotous scene, complete with Furlow's eight whippets, a six-foot-by-eight-foot aviary filled with dozens of chirping finches and weavers, and Furlow and John at the center of things, finding or creating gorgeous must-have pieces. At one point, when all the whippets went missing, John went so far as to call the police. Hours later they emerged from an enormous armoire where they'd been napping atop piles of linens. "It was a wild scene," Bob says. "And a great education."

In New York, Furlow began collecting in earnest, for the shop and for himself. He combed every sale, visited every old house, turned up at every country auction. He also began regular runs between Manhattan and Georgia, where he bought things for the business—journeys he finally quit making at ninety. But he still drives the three-hour trek to Scott's Antiques Market in Atlanta each month, and he rarely returns empty-handed.

While Furlow is one of the greatest designers I've ever encountered, his is hardly a traditional approach. Just as the design of an entire house might begin with a set of French doors, his method with regard to the interiors is equally idiosyncratic. "In decorating," says Bunny, "you start with a rug and fabric. Furlow buys furniture and he may come back from India with a bolt of cloth." It's certainly true that fabric houses would never get rich off him. There is not a single curtain in any of his houses—he much prefers shutters or blinds. The bulk of his upholstered furniture is slipcovered in simple cotton duck, and rugs, when they exist at all, are sisal or Indian dhurries or the odd antique Oriental. But the most salient quality of his "look" is that he only buys what he absolutely loves; a purchase is never made with an eye toward period or, God forbid, toward what matches or "goes with" another piece. "In the Peacock House, for example, you have this early Italian table and a French Directoire chair and a William and Mary Dutch chandelier," says Bunny. "Most people don't have the courage to do that."

Furlow's love of animals goes at least as far back as his love of collecting. As a child, one of his earliest pets was a chicken named Blackie. "I used to roller-skate with him," he tells me. "I'd put

a rag over his head and rock him to sleep." During an entire summer Furlow spent with an aunt in Florida, Blackie "went wild," his mother told him later, so she had no choice but to chop off his head and have him for supper. "It's the only thing I hold against my mother."

While that story might accurately come under the heading of "Southern Gothic," there is nothing remotely gothic about Furlow except his great love of the architecture of that period. But before our first meeting, I was skeptical, having heard the tales of a mad-sounding collector with his peacocks and dogs and ever-burgeoning collection of houses and things. But Furlow is neither mad nor a member of that breed I most abhor, the professional "Southern Character." What he is instead is a Southern gentleman in the true sense of the word, beautifully mannered, funny and smart and kind, a great character but without the quotation marks.

Finally, for all of Furlow's knowledge, for all his world travels and world-class stuff, he has never been a snob. One of my very favorite things in the whole Barn is on the drinks tray outside the bedroom where I slept. A blue liner, it fit perfectly inside a handsome silver urn that doubles as an ice bucket, and I assumed it was some fine piece of cobalt glass. Upon further inspection, it was a plastic bowl Furlow said he found at the Dollar Store, a detail that delighted him to repeat.

Because in the end, Furlow's world is not remotely about provenance or pretension. It is an eminently comfortable, welcoming space put together by a lovely man with an extraordinary eye: A place where pets are at least as pampered as the people, where in the kitchen you can always find a cookie tray of dog food on the floor and a cookie tin of cheese straws on the counter. When we left after that first visit, Henry whimpered the whole way out of Americus. He was speaking for both of us.

CHAPTER I

THE BARN

The Barn, the first of Furlow's "follies," was not actually a folly at all, but a rescue mission and longtime labor of love. In the 1950s, during one of Furlow's frequent visits home from New York—to see his mother and forage for antiques for the store—he noticed that the carriage house on the property was on the brink of collapse. "It had gotten to the point where it had to be restored or torn down," he says. "So every time I had a couple of extra hundred dollars, I'd send them to a carpenter and have him do some work on the place."

The original structure had a large center room with a wing off each side. One of the wings, home to Furlow's current living room, was where the carriages were kept—they entered through the three big spaces now covered by custom-made French doors. The other, part of which now includes Furlow's bedroom, contained the stalls; hay was sent down through a chute from the loft above.

The first additions, two enclosed "porches" attached to the front and back of the central room, allowed him to leave the space's two enormous archways intact. He then expanded the area that became the kitchen and added bay windows, and built a long dining room off the living room, which was given more elaborate bay windows with Gothic fretwork. Bedroom wings were added on each side. "Whenever I'd buy too much furniture," Furlow says, not entirely in jest, "I'd have to add a room."

In the course of all the Barn's renovations and additions, Furlow established the themes that would recur as other structures were built or landed on the property. The Gothic fretwork in the dining room, for example, previews the predominately Gothic architecture and decorative elements of the future "follies." The walls are neutral (with the exception of the charming "blue room" and the cantaloupe-colored center room), and the window treatments are dead simple. (Furlow prefers shutters or the kitchen's wooden blinds that are similar, he says, to "those that everyone in the South had on their screened porches in the thirties and forties.")

Furlow relaxing on the back porch of the Barn. A circular stair in the adjacent original center room leads to a space containing the heating units and storage.

And then, of course, there is the introduction of architectural elements—from the simple to the extraordinary—that define and uplift the space.

Some, like the mirrors with fanlights that mimic windows in the center room, were designed by Furlow and John Rosselli and made at the shop. Others, like the magnificent eighteenth-century Italian door in Furlow's bedroom, were bought at a country auction. The door is also a prime example of the lengths to which Furlow will go to get things right. "When I bought that door, it had five thousand coats of white paint on it," he says, laughing. Undeterred, he welded two 250-gallon drums together in the low-ceilinged basement below the 72nd Street shop, filled the resulting receptacle with potash, and dropped pieces of the door inside—over and over again. "You could do anything in New York in those days, but if the Health Department had come or anyone had fallen into that drum, it would have been hell."

Probably, but the risk was well worth it. "It doesn't matter if you're into architecture or decoration, when you walk into that Barn, you're bowled over," says decorative painter Bob Christian. "It's just a visual feast."

The center room's dining chairs were strapped to the top of Furlow's Dodge Dart and driven from New York, while the shutters were discovered in a house being torn down in New Jersey.

The enclosed porch in
the front also serves as an
entrance hall. Guests are
met at the door by a pair
of stag's heads. One is
wooden, one fiberglass, and
both have real horns.

The natural boards of the front porch's walls are reflected in the rest of the room's neutral color
scheme, and the furniture is the usual fearless Furlow mix, including a rush-bottomed bench,
a French sofa, and two consoles made by Furlow's contractor and builder, Jimmy Fuller.
Jimmy also made the round drop-leaf center table, which was then painted by Bob Christian.

A view through the French doors of the dining room, also known as the "glass room,"
out to the "chapel," which is mostly used for tools. The long rectangular space was
added off the living room and given a huge bay window with Gothic fretwork
designed by Furlow. A wood pagoda and a pair of carved wood cranes anchor the back.

On the left, custom French doors lead from the Barn's living room into the dining room. Above, Kitty lounges in front of one of the dining room's floor-to-ceiling windows. The potted Australian tree ferns are moved inside from the garden in winter.

The antique Chinese dish was designed for watercolorists, with a slot for fresh water on one side and already mixed paint on the other. Furlow says he regrets that he didn't buy more. Like most of the Barn, the living room walls here and on the following two spreads are comprised of rough boards covered with water-based white paint. The Dutch cupboard has a similar finish.

The living room mantel's hearth surround is composed of tiles that Bunny Williams and John Rosselli had made in Italy, and which complement Furlow's vast collection of blue-and-white porcelain.
The painting above the mantel was bought at auction (on the back, someone had scrawled "The Gould Children") and the rug is an Indian dhurrie. The fabulous stag chair was purchased at Sotheby's.

Furlow added this bedroom wing, comprised of a spacious hall, bedroom, and bath, to the Barn's original structure. He bought the marble bust of a boy in Savannah, where he once owned a house.

This bedroom, in the wing pictured on the previous pages, features a giant tapestry cartoon—the life-size model from which a tapestry was woven—above the four-poster antique bed. Furlow found the brackets, painted them white, and placed them at strategic points around the room to lend bits of architecture to the otherwise fairly rustic space.

Portrait of Phillip on the
back porch. The Indian
sofa and pillow fabrics are
mostly bedspreads and the
painting above is a copy of
an antique Indian wallpaper
panel. The book, *Les Chiens,*
was a gift from Bunny
Williams and John Rosselli.

48

Furlow's bedroom boasts
the Barn's only important
cornice, which puts the
room's eighteenth-century
door (page 50) in fine
proportion. The four-
poster bed was his mother's
and is hung with antique
toile de Jouy.

It's a dog's life: The four dogs have the run of the Barn, and sweet Phillip is often found nestled in his master's well-appointed bed. The desk at the bed's foot contains a typically seductive mix of Furlow's treasures, including a tortoiseshell and ivory English tea caddy in the shape of a house.

The tiny "blue room" is original to the Barn, but the marvelous blue paneling itself, as well as the unstained floors, came from an old tenant house on the Hodges farm near Americus.

The vast guest room, also featured on the previous pages, was an addition to the original structure. A desk contains two books that sum up the extremes of Furlow's interests: *John Fowler, Prince of Decorators* by Martin Wood and *White Trash Cooking* by Ernest Matthew Mickler. The wooden deer is a copy of a bronze one found in Pompeii.

In the sunny kitchen, Furlow makes his famous cheese straws, which he totes to New York on still-frequent visits. Above the sink, narrow shelves show off more of his collection of blue-and-white porcelain. In order to display the three pitchers in front of the platters, Furlow fashioned ingenious wooden "paddles," which he attached by screwing their "handles" underneath the shelves.

Above, Phillip takes up one of his many usual posts in front of the kitchen window. Opposite and on the following spread is the table where Furlow most often dines. He added the bay window when he enlarged the kitchen, and ordered the old-fashioned wooden blinds from DeVenco, a company in Atlanta that has been manufacturing them for more than seventy years. Typical of Furlow, the furniture around the table is ever shifting—the Chippendale sofa, left, currently resides in the Lumpkin House.

CHAPTER II

THE PEACOCK HOUSE

Before it became a full-fledged house with a bedroom, bath, kitchen, and back porch, the Peacock House began life as a winter plant repository with dirt floors. But, like so many of Furlow's "follies," its real reason for being was to make use of three fabulous sets of French doors (found years earlier at New York's Pier Antiques Show), an egg-and-dart front door (from a house "somewhere" on the Hudson), and columns copied from a pair found in Atlanta, at Scott's Antiques Market.

Enter Joe McElroy, Furlow's carpenter of almost twenty years, who explains the house's beginnings with a spot-on imitation of the boss's deadpan instructions: "Joe, I want you to build me a house around this door."

The doorframe's Gothic window inspired the porch's fretwork, a pattern Furlow had Joe copy from an image in a book on Gothic houses, while the slightly more rustic arrows pointing upward are, says Furlow, "sort of carpenter Gothic." The French doors were installed to create pretty much the entire back wall of the one-room "house," and, in an especially ingenious space-saving move, were made to pivot from the center rather than to open flat.

Despite the light afforded by the doors, the plants, apparently, weren't happy in their fine abode. Roosts and nesting boxes were then installed for the next tenants, the peacocks, but they too were unhappy—the "runway" wasn't long enough, which meant that they most often hit the rafters when they tried to fly out.

As it happens, the house's failed beginnings as a utilitarian space are what made the final version so utterly chic and seductive. "The wall makes the whole thing," Furlow says. "If we hadn't started with a single room, we wouldn't have had this wall of doors." Indeed, the doors likely would have been split up to make entrances to more than one room, say, or one big room would have been created without the doors down the middle. Instead, Joe simply tacked on an identical room to the existing one, along with a wing on each side, one for a bed and bath, and one for a kitchen. The "door wall" that remained lends definition and architecture to the space while still allowing light to flow through.

Still life with rifle and box lock: The antique brass lock is the kind of thing Furlow has by the drawer full. Bob Christian painted the floor's Greek key border.

Though the interior walls are the simple painted boards Furlow prefers, further architecture was added in the form of: another pair of French doors with fanlights that serve as entrances to the bed and kitchen wings; the Greek key borders on Bob Christian's gorgeous painted floors; an important looking cornice; and a pair of William Kent-ish mirrors designed by Furlow and John Rosselli. The focal point, a mantel found in a house near Cold Spring, New York, is, says Bunny, "the most beautiful mantel ever," while Furlow himself refers to it fondly as his "little money-maker." Years ago, he explains, it was bought by Prince Faisal, who "went broke" and sold it back to him for one tenth of the price.

As always, it's Furlow's singular eye for the decorative detail that puts the house over the top. Painted wrought-iron vents, usually found in the brick foundations of Victorian houses, here flank the French door fanlights, for example. The portrait hanging in a place of honor above the fireplace had been banished until Furlow replaced the Victorian frame with its current one, and now, he says, "It's super." Even the already superb mantel below got a boost: a horrified Joe was ordered to paint the mahogany spindles so that Bob could "gray up" the whole thing, and a pair of porcelain plates with stags was affixed to it. "I'm always good at goosing things up," Furlow says, with typical understatement. The evolution of the Peacock House from failed greenhouse to perfect jewel box is a perfect case in point.

The house's gray and white paint colors serve as the perfect background for Furlow's extensive collections of blue-and-white porcelains and fabrics. Bob Christian painted the formerly dark mahogany mantel, while the porcelain plates affixed to it look as though they were made for the piece. The gilded peacock bellows was found on one of Furlow's many trips to India.

The "stones" surrounding
the hearth are French
terra-cotta roof tiles. The
console tables on each
side were copied from a
magazine photo and the oft-
used painted metal fronds
above were designed by
Furlow and made in India.

The bust in the front room is one of a pair Furlow found in England, and the oil of Diana, goddess of the hunt, was bought at auction. The mix of fabrics is typical Furlow: Robert Kime Susani Yellow with white duck, a simple check, and a faded linen print. The gray wooden blinds from DeVenco are similar to those found in the Barn's kitchen.

The entrance to the
sleeping wing is flanked by
mirrors designed by Furlow
and John Rosselli. In the
foreground, a Billy Baldwin
slipper chair is covered
in fabric on the wrong side,
a favorite Furlow trick.

Mirrored French doors lead into a bath with a linen press and an ikat-covered wicker chair.
In the tiny bedroom, framed pieces of old toile decorate the walls; the bed and table are
from John Rosselli. On the following pages, Furlow bought most of the fretwork for
the back porch from Connecticut dealer Michael Trapp and had his carpenter copy the rest.

CHAPTER III

THE CUTHBERT HOUSE

Furlow had been eyeballing the Cuthbert House, a mid-nineteenth-century Gothic Revival dwelling located in nearby Cuthbert, Georgia, for decades. But it wasn't until 2007, when he learned that it was about to be demolished by the local Methodist church to make way for a parking lot, that he went into action. Clearly, he's mystified by the congregation's logic: "There are only about twenty-five members," he says, in his inimitable deadpan. "Surely they could have parked on the street." But the church's disinterest in the building's gorgeous architecture was Furlow's great gain.

As soon as the house made the sixty-five-mile journey—in two major pieces—and was set into its new concrete foundation, Furlow and his über-talented builder, Jimmy Fuller, got to work. "It was pretty much there," says Jimmy, meaning that the only additions the pair made to the existing structure were a kitchen, a back porch, and a bath for the first-floor bedroom. More important, it had remarkable bones: sixteen-foot ceilings, fourteen-foot windows, perfect symmetry, and a wide center hall with a columned archway.

Furlow, charmed by the beveled pieces of wood on the front porch, which had been cut and laid out to mimic stone, asked Jimmy to reproduce the same effect in the interior hall. Unhappy with the short, narrow doors that led from the hall into the identical living rooms on each side, he directed Jimmy to replace them by copying the hall's archway. Both living rooms got a wall of bookshelves and mantels with mirrored overmantels. The stairway was lacking a banister and railings, so Furlow designed those as well.

All of the changes, as is the usual case with these design partners, were mapped out in shorthand conversation and on scraps of paper. "He'll do a little hand-sketch and then I'll take it and scale it down to make it work," Jimmy says. "Or a lot of times we'll just be standing there talking, and he'll tell me something, and it'll just click. There's nothing formal about it." Maybe not, but in the case of the Cuthbert House, the end result is grand indeed. "It's got that high-

end neoclassical look Furlow loves," says Jimmy. "But he always adds something to the mix." The stair railings, for example, are almost Chippendale, and the mirrored French doors in the dining room add a decided touch of glamour.

The house, which was completed in an astonishing eighteen months, shares the same gray and white interior paint scheme as the Peacock House and Lumpkin House, and Furlow's collection of blue-and-white china is represented here in earnest. But like all of his "follies," the Cuthbert House is possessed of its own distinct personality and considerable charms, not least of which is the spacious, lattice-columned back porch. It is also by far the most formal structure on the property, which is reflected by bits of the decor. The only crystal chandelier Furlow owns hangs in the dining room, and an imposing statue of Diana, goddess of the hunt, dominates the hall. But with Furlow, there's always an endearing, humanizing quirk: The deer accompanying Diana is missing its head and much of its torso.

The statue of Diana, goddess of the hunt, is especially fitting. Furlow is certainly
master of the hunt for beautiful things and extraordinary houses, but the two share
another trait: Diana also was said to be able to talk to and control animals. To her left,
a pair of blue-and-white urns flanks the open French doors to the dining room.

Furlow asked his builder, Jimmy Fuller, to make the doorways from the dining room into one of the living rooms deeper so that he could install the gray and white painted panels. Furlow also came up with the pullout "table" beneath the bookshelves and designed the custom-made shutters for the tall living room windows.

Part of Furlow's collection of pagodas adorns the dining table. The table, chairs, console, and candlesticks are all from John Rosselli. Manhattan-based painter John Campbell painted the faux marbre floors, and a grisaille wallpaper panel hangs above the console. A similar gray palate (with white) extends throughout the house. Furlow says he finds the color scheme cooling.

Two identically proportioned front living rooms are entered through expansive archways from the center hall. In the one on the right, a nineteenth-century oil painting of a greyhound hangs over the mirrored overmantel, which was designed by Furlow. Phillip strikes an elegant pose on the Louis VI–style ottoman from John Rosselli, upholstered in white cotton duck.

To create sofas for the two front living rooms, Furlow added backs to a pair of French daybeds. Both rooms feature sisal rugs from Stark, as well as the metal wall fronds Furlow had made in India. On page 120, a view from the first-floor bedroom shows a console in the hall, to the right of a door leading into the dining room. In the room on page 121, the fronds hang above a nineteenth-century Regency convex bull's-eye mirror, rather than the trumeau pictured here.

The spacious back porch was added to the house and features louvered shutters between
latticework columns. A birdcage from Furlow's collection sits atop a table fashioned
from a wicker tray and a faux grapevine base. The rug is an Indian dhurrie and the John
Robshaw red-and-white pillow fabric is also used on the table in the next spread.

One of the three second-floor bedrooms gets an antique French bed topped with blue-
and-white toile lined in yellow. The first-floor bedroom is graced with an even grander piece,
a camel-bone and teak four-poster from John Rosselli. The prints are Audubon and the
nightstand with its hidden cabinet was designed by Furlow and also made at Rosselli.

The antique bed in another upstairs bedroom once belonged to Bunny Williams—Furlow sold it to her but she traded it back years later. Furlow says the dealer from whom he bought the cupboard in the third upstairs bedroom insisted it was old, but he knew better. He bought it, as he does so many things, because he liked its looks. The tufted chairs are Victorian.

The two black-and-white photographs are of members of some of Furlow's previous dog families. In one of the two second-floor bathrooms, both the hand-carved Regency-style mirror and sink are from John Rosselli. The screen features trompe l'oeil paintings of pigeons.

CHAPTER IV

THE LUMPKIN HOUSE

In 2010, Furlow was told about a charming, uninhabited house in neighboring Stewart County, so he and his friend and builder Jimmy Fuller went off in search of it during one of their many countryside drives. It turned out that the house, near the little town of Lumpkin (population 2,000), was owned by a cousin of Furlow's cousin—a not-unusual Southern state of affairs that greatly facilitated the deal.

"I think I really bought it for the front door and the gingerbread on the front porch," Furlow says, an assessment Jimmy backs up. "When we first saw it, he said, 'Jimmy, this is one of the most beautiful door units I've ever seen,' and of course I had to agree."

So it was that the Lumpkin House was put on a truck and toted forty miles to Americus, where it took up residence catty-cornered across a lane of sorts from the Cuthbert House. Since it was a less complicated structure—essentially a one-story center-hall cottage with two rooms on each side—it also was less of an ordeal to move. As soon as it was set down on its concrete block foundation, one of the first tasks was installing a floor in the kitchen. (Furlow has modernized each of the kitchens in his "follies," complete with sleek appliances that are rarely touched.) Next up, the drywall was stripped down to the planked walls, which, in the hall and living rooms, retain their original paint, worn to a perfect patina.

The house also provided an opportunity for Furlow to utilize some of the many architectural elements that fill up his pigeon houses cum storage sheds. The dining area at the end of the center hall was given a more auspicious entrance courtesy of a pair of found Ionic columns, and the space was moved back a few feet so that a rather grand Palladian window could be installed. The window itself is a glorious hodgepodge—part window and part door. "I'd had the broken pediment and the doorway stashed away for years," Furlow says, adding that he "robbed" his bathroom at the Barn of its window so he could complete the center hall. It was also missing two of its six columns, so Jimmy (after telling Furlow what it would cost to replace them with wood versions) arrived at a clever substitute. "We used PVC pipe instead," Jimmy says, laughing at their shared "creativity."

The center hall leads into the dining area, which has a kitchen to the left and a bedroom and bath to the right. The stacks of creamware on the dining table are from the same set that is displayed on the room's wall on pages 141 and 155.

Furlow reports that the stunning front door, pictured left, before it received its current paint job, is the feature that convinced him to buy the structure. Opposite is a view of the rear of the house, not long after it made the trip from Lumpkin, Georgia. The Palladian window opposite, made of a hodgepodge of architectural elements, was installed in the space covered by the tarp in the photograph.

Since the color scheme is the same gray and white found in the Peacock House and Cuthbert Houses, Bob Christian had been instructed to create another version of the painted Peacock House floors in the hall. "I think I already had the paint with me," Bob says. "Then Furlow showed up and pulled two pictures of a villa in Italy out of his pocket." The floors in the photographs had a design in red tile, so the Lumpkin floors also became a fabulous deep red, offset by a Greek key border. In one fell swoop, Bob says, "We went from Sweden to Italy."

The rest of the floors are a simple stained heart pine and, as always, rugs are kept to a minimum. Likewise, the windows all remain bare—though there is no shortage of the usual trove of treasures placed throughout. A marvelous collection of creamware is displayed on brackets on one wall of the dining room. In one of the living rooms, a rare set of four European botanicals frames the doorway. "They were once used in classrooms," Furlow says, "to teach the children about horticulture."

The end result is another triumph, but when I ask Furlow if he ever wanders over, he says, "If I told you I do, I'd be lying." The pleasure, as he has said many times before, is in "the doing." Again, Jimmy Fuller echoes his friend's sentiments. "As soon as he's through doing business with you on one project, he's ready to move on." The rest of us, though, remained dazzled by each creation, including the Lumpkin House, his last (so far). Says Jimmy Fuller, "You walk in and you just can't believe you're in Americus, Sumter County, Georgia."

Bob Christian, above, top left, painted the hall floors a deep-red pattern inspired by a magazine photo Furlow found of a house in Italy. His assistant, Michael Carnahan, bottom right, draws off the pattern, which includes a Greek key border. Opposite, a marble statue of a woman keeps watch outside the dining room window.

The swan-necked broken pediment is one of the elements that make up the dining room window. The tole mechanical bird toy that sits beneath the curve is an example of the tiny treasures Furlow likes to place in unexpected spots.

Above, Furlow reads in one of the two Lumpkin House living rooms. Opposite, clockwise from top left: Bob Christian created the trompe l'oeil dove perched atop the doorway that leads from the dining room into the kitchen; a bracket adorns one of the beautifully aged planked walls, discovered when the drywall was peeled away; Bob Christian gave the pair of neoclassical consoles, designed by Furlow for the center hall, a subtle Greek key pattern that echoes the painted floor's border.

The pillows on a slipcovered living room sofa above and on the previous spread are covered in a mix of fabrics ranging from Robert Kime and old Fortuny to a simple check. Opposite, the sofa is Swedish, and the Regency-style chair in the foreground from John Rosselli is covered in Nympheous from GP & J Baker, a pattern Furlow used in the Peacock House, but on the "wrong" side.

Furlow is notoriously
fearless when it comes to
mixing styles and periods.
A simple wicker porch chair
covered in blue-and-white
ticking shares space with a
pair of "French" armchairs
from John Rosselli and
an antique Swedish desk
topped with a rooster.

A view across the center hall to the identical living room. The European botanical prints, now quite rare, were once used to teach schoolchildren about horticulture. The doors and their knobs are original to the house. The watercolor of tulips on page 158 is by Hazard Durfee.

One of Furlow's favorite camellias, the Frank Houser, sits in a blue-and-white porcelain
dish. The bedroom contains a beguiling mix of high and low: A reproduction of a
cow hangs above an Old Paris compote on the mantel, the rug is an Indian dhurrie,
and the antique French bed is covered by a graphic antique quilt found at auction.

CHAPTER V

THE GARDENS & OUTBUILDINGS

Furlow is as unreflective about how, exactly, he laid out the eleven acres on which his houses sit as he is about the rest of his magical creations. "It just happened," he says. Also, like a lot of Southerners of his generation, he is firm about the fact that the property is a "yard" rather than a "garden."

He has a point on both fronts. There was never a long-term, drawn-up landscaping plan—the grounds evolved as the number of houses and outbuildings grew. And though there are dozens of plant varieties, including concentrations of more than a thousand daffodil and narcissus bulbs and masses of white butterfly ginger lilies, there are no gardens in the proper sense. As he did everywhere else, Furlow relied on his remarkable sense of proportion. More important, he simply planted what he loves.

Since the property itself is on part of what used to be his family's farm, there are still the majestic remnants of the pecan groves, once so common in the area. An existing allée of the trees was made far more dramatic with underplantings of dozens of crape myrtle bushes and another "allée" of twenty-six hydrangeas in clay pots. The rest of the plant material is similarly Southern: enormous oaks in which the peacocks roost at night; pear trees and old-fashioned "sugar" figs; azaleas and old roses; and camellias, including Furlow's two favorites, the Queen Bee and the Frank Houser, a hybrid that originated in Macon, Georgia.

Three of the outbuildings are especially typical of Southern homes of a more gracious era: a pair of pigeonniers or pigeon houses, which in this case contain garden tools and architectural fragments; and a chicken house, which currently serves as a hospital for injured peacocks. The pigeonniers came into being a few years ago after Furlow found a pair of fanlights he loved and promptly designed two structures around them. The chicken house, also of Furlow's design, was once home to fifty Japanese Bantam chickens, a mostly ornamental and notably amiable breed that has graced aristocratic Japanese gardens for more than 350 years. They were ensconced in Furlow's own place for a little over two—until, he says, he "got bored with them" and gave them away.

Furlow watering one of his citrus pots on the terrace outside the back porch of the Barn. Pears are among the fruit trees found on the property. The others are fig, pomegranate, orange, lemon, and grapefruit.

The peacocks are unlikely to meet a similar fate. About a decade or so ago, Furlow became enchanted by a pair kept by his nephew, Jimbo Gatewood, who lives in Furlow's mother's former house next door. "That got me started," he says, and since then he's acquired an ever-growing brood that now numbers more than forty. That's a lot of birds, but it is precisely this kind of volume—of birds, of plants, of charming garden ornaments and outbuildings—that makes the "yard" so special. "I think Furlow lives for interesting scale," says Bob Christian. "When most people would put in six hydrangeas, he will plant forty. Or he'll say, 'Let's go put in six hundred bulbs this afternoon.'"

No matter what he adds, the components are invariably harmonious. It helps that there are so many mature boxwoods available for transplanting in front of the more recently added structures and that most of the buildings are of the same regional vernacular. "He is not trying to do Williamsburg down there," says Bob. "Everything looks like it should be exactly where it is. And that it has been there forever."

Among the ornaments scattered throughout the property is a wooden
deer head, which is attached to the Barn. Its antlers were eaten off by squirrels.
An antique urn containing a cedar is nestled among ferns and azaleas.

The chicken house was once home to fifty Japanese Bantam chickens and now serves as a peacock hospital. On the previous spread, an antique French stone fountain covered in fig ivy is positioned just off the pea-gravel drive in front of the Barn. Irises and hydrangeas are planted in the bed behind it.

Another antique French fountain provides a perch for one of the peacocks. The clay pots contain Australian tree ferns. Furlow transfers them into the Barn's "glass room," also known as the dining room, during the winter months.

Furlow's "snowball" tree is in stunning full bloom outside the Lumpkin House, above. On the right, white agapanthus are planted in the boxes outside one of the pair of pigeon houses Furlow designed on the property. The columns are copies of those on the front porch of the Peacock House.

Furlow designed the Gothic "chapel, " which has a French stone floor and
interiors painted by Bob Christian, who reports that Furlow told him to be sure
to have some things flying on the walls.

CHAPTER VI

COLLECTIONS

In the more than eight decades since Furlow made his first purchase—the milk glass chickens he bought with earnings from his childhood paper route—he has amassed impressive collections of everything, from porcelain and pagodas to birdcages and buildings.

But Furlow is hardly a collector in the traditional sense. He has never bought a single piece of art or furniture, book or bibelot with an eye toward future value. Nor is it about the quest for the very best of anything. If he sees something that strikes his fancy, he buys it. Then, he says, when he runs across more of the same, he buys that too.

Furlow may be typically succinct when describing his collecting strategy, or lack thereof, but there is nothing typical about his eye. "He always goes toward the most unusual example of something," says John, who has spent countless hours shopping alongside him. "Nothing he chooses is ordinary."

There are themes, of course. He has always been mad for architectural elements—and especially intrepid about procuring them. Once, years ago, a set of doors he was transporting from New Jersey across the George Washington Bridge flew off the top of his car and landed in the Hudson River. "I was very lucky that they didn't kill somebody," Furlow says. "There were holes in the roof where they took the luggage rack with them."

And then there is the porcelain: the ubiquitous blue and white and countless Chinese figures, but also troves of Old Paris, including five sets of pots de crème, a substantial set of Wedding Band (white with a gold rim), and an even larger one of peach and white. "He does it little by little, which is the only way," says Bunny. "One New Year's Day, he had a party with forty people and we all ate off the peach-and-white service, three courses, and the table was decorated with it too."

For a time, the dining table in the Cuthbert House was covered in a fine old piece of Fortuny, but there is nothing highbrow about his collection of fabrics. Indian bedspreads, old

The milk glass compotes were the very first antiques Furlow bought. The elaborate chinoiserie secretary is new, but Furlow plans to "age" the patina with steel wool. The piece holds many "recurring" treasures, ranging from blue-and-white porcelain to leather-bound books.

and new toile, ticking, and simple gingham checks live harmoniously with a few yards here and there from the most esteemed designers. "I have everything from Robert Kime to dish towels," he says, "And let me tell you, a dish towel can make a very nice pillow."

When asked to name some of Furlow's favorites, John is as equivocal as his friend. "I wish I could say there was something in particular that he was always fascinated with. Pagodas are one—he was very much taken with the Brighton Royal Pavilion. But really, he loves beautiful things across the board." Furlow himself concurs, "You know what, I really like everything."

It is clear that he also likes the chase, the discovery of something that can still surprise him, something perfect to enhance his ever-expanding spaces. A few months after the Lumpkin House was "finished," Furlow found a 140-piece set of blue-and-white English transferware in Atlanta at Scott's (which he invariably refers to as "the flea market"). After a bit of haggling—and Furlow's subsequent departure, empty-handed—the dealer phoned later with a more attractive price. Now the set, complete with every possible serving piece, graces the house's formerly pristine kitchen. "It's so exquisite you can't believe it," says John. And, doubtless, exactly what the room needed.

A tole pagoda John Rosselli once produced in bulk in China sits atop a table on the back porch
of the Peacock House and holds tiny porcelain critters. On the back porch of the Cuthbert House,
two antique Gothic corner tables create a demilune console, where a Gothic church spire
has pride of place. The candlesticks and the trompe l'oeil bird painting also are from Rosselli.

More of Furlow's beloved blue-and-white porcelain and a Chinese export platter sit atop
a long antique Gothic sideboard in the back porch of the Barn. On the previous
spread, there are examples of the horn and tortoiseshell pieces that Furlow collects in all
forms, along with new white porcelain shellfish and a Victorian figurine of a whippet.

Furlow's immense collection of Old Paris porcelain includes a peach-and-white service
with enough pieces for a three-course dinner for forty. The exquisite set of pots de crème
is one of five that he owns. The day lily and gardenia blossoms are from the garden.

A kitchen drawer holds piles of the American coin silver Furlow has collected over many decades in two primary patterns, Sheaf of Wheat and Basket of Flowers. The latter is his favorite.

CHAPTER VII

LESSONS LEARNED

BY BUNNY WILLIAMS

Furlow Gatewood was born with an extraordinary eye and a passion for architecture and interior design. He directed that passion into a career as an antiques dealer, and has told me many times that he would never have had the patience to work with clients. But his very personal approach to design can be seen in his "laboratory" of sorts—the four remarkable houses on his property in Americus. Even though Furlow is a traditionalist, his houses always seem alive, never staid. One of his strongest hallmarks is a grand sense of scale. The tall doors and windows, the gutsy pieces of furniture that almost touch the ceiling—all contribute to the excitement of being in each space. The following are lessons that everyone can learn from studying these unique houses.

Furlow often uses simple rough boards as panels for a room. This gives texture and character that plain drywall cannot provide. In some cases, the boards run vertically with horizontal boards at the ceiling, chair rail, and base. Some of the rooms have traditional board-and-batten detail, which can make them even taller.

The stylish entrance hall of the Cuthbert House was created by simply cutting pieces of plywood in six-by-twenty-inch rectangles. The edges of each piece of wood were beveled and installed in a running bond pattern over the drywall. This was a technique often used in American nineteenth-century Federal houses to simulate stone patterns, as dwellings were then built of wood.

Furlow is always on the hunt for fabulous architectural elements. Period mantels of extraordinary quality were found for the Barn and the Peacock House. A great eighteenth-century pine Georgian door surround looks majestic in his bedroom in the Barn. The porch of the Peacock House began with the purchase of two Gothic columns he copied and used again in the pigeon houses that were themselves built around two antique fanlight windows. The design for the Peacock House's back porch came after he bought bits of unusual lattice in Connecticut. Old painted boards were incorporated into the small "blue room" in the Barn. Everywhere, the bits of architecture he may have found in a salvage yard serve to inspire or improve.

In each living room, the furniture is always arranged in comfortable seating groups consisting of large frame sofas and various frame chairs placed around them. He often implements period sofas and chairs with exposed legs to give the rooms a light, airy quality. The chairs almost dance

206

A mid-nineteenth-century mirrored trellis on the back porch of the Peacock House was an inspiration for the mirrors with similar fanlights in the Barn. On the previous page are the brilliant "paddles" Furlow affixed to the Lumpkin House bookshelves in order to support a pair of lamps from John Rosselli.

across the floors, which allows for easy movement should another last-minute seat be needed to fill out a grouping. Generous upholstered pieces are used sparingly. Large tables are added to hold lamps next to sofas, and small tables are scattered about so that a cup of tea or glass of wine can be set down within easy reach.

Paintings, mirrors, plates, brackets, and sconces are arranged on the walls in the most wonderful way. Some walls have large pictures or mirrors, while others are covered with combinations of small pictures that are stacked one atop the other, with a bracket above to draw the eye up and accentuate the sense of grandeur.

Each piece of furniture that catches Furlow's eye—whether he's wandering through an antiques fair or stopping at a junk shop along a country road—has unusual character. A hoof, a foot, a carved shell, a beautiful faded crotch mahogany panel, or a worn and faded painted finish are the sorts of details that will grab his attention. His collection consists of American, English, French, Swedish, and Italian pieces spanning many centuries. Individual pieces have soul and character; he combines them in such a way so that each stands out. Painted furniture sits next to a mellow wood piece. A large English mahogany armchair is placed next to a painted French chair

with a cabriole leg. The groupings are never boring or obvious; rather they are always unexpected. Sometimes Furlow will find a great piece of second-hand furniture of a fabulous design but bad wood and say, "This would look great painted white." And the piece is immediately transformed. He is not a purist, and that is what makes his houses have such a sense of fantasy.

One thing I am sure of is that no fabric house is going to get rich off Furlow's purchase of materials. There are no curtains in the houses and most of the large sofas are covered in a solid fabric and then filled with pillows of different florals, stripes, and checks in a single color scheme. Blue-and-white fabrics are used throughout to complement his collection of blue-and-white china. A single chair might have a patterned fabric that blends with the others. Furlow also has the most amazing eye for combining various fabrics. The many red-and-white hand-blocked fabrics that cover the large sofa in the Barn are a symphony of shades and patterns.

If a chair has lovely old leather upholstery, it is left as is. Furlow will find a few yards of a vintage Fortuny fabric or a lovely faded chintz remnant for cushions. Bedrooms might have an American patchwork quilt over the foot of the bed. Soft, mellow Oriental rugs provide warmth and large antique blue-and-white striped cotton Indian dhurries add a seemingly modern touch.

Furlow loves old china, silver, and glass, but since full sets are often very expensive and hard to come by, he has amassed wonderful sets over many years, as in his many sets of Old Paris. Furlow loves coin silver, as do I, and he has put together the most amazing set in the Sheaf of Wheat and Basket of Flowers patterns. The pieces work so wonderfully together.

Throughout Furlow's houses there are the most creative solutions to solving problems. As there is almost never enough light near bookcases, Furlow had round wooden disks constructed with "handles" (much like paddles) and attached them to the bottom of some of the shelves. On two such disks in the Lumpkin House, he added lovely ivory candlestick lamps. When designing the bookcases in the Cuthbert House, he had pullout shelves added at table height to hold a lamp or other objects.

As storage is always a problem, Furlow designed wonderful ribbed wooden octagonal columns, inspired by Edwardian cabinets, which were made to conceal chamber pots in a tasteful way. In these, a discreet door swings open to reveal the shelves inside. They are perfect as bedside tables or in bathrooms to hold toiletries and towels.

Furlow's homes and "follies" are exceptional to be sure. But what puts them into a category by themselves is that they were created by an entirely self-taught designer. The real lesson learned from this supremely gifted man is to educate your eye and look at the best of everything, be it architecture, furniture, or design. And may you too have the joy that Furlow has had over the many years of doing what he loves.

John Rosselli says that Furlow has always been drawn to pieces with strong "personality." Here, the distinctive feet on pieces of furniture throughout his houses provide lots of it. The two previous spreads feature the fluted cabinets Furlow designed for Rosselli (page 211) and architectural details from the Cuthbert House (page 212) and the Peacock House (page 213).

Above and opposite: The greatest lesson learned from Furlow is that no house is complete without a menagerie—and that decoration should never be so precious that it intimidates animals or people! Kitty wanders across the damask-covered table in the Barn's dining room. Furlow cuddles with Will and Phillip; Phillip strikes two more poses; and Henry, the visiting beagle, finds a sunlit spot in the Barn's back porch.

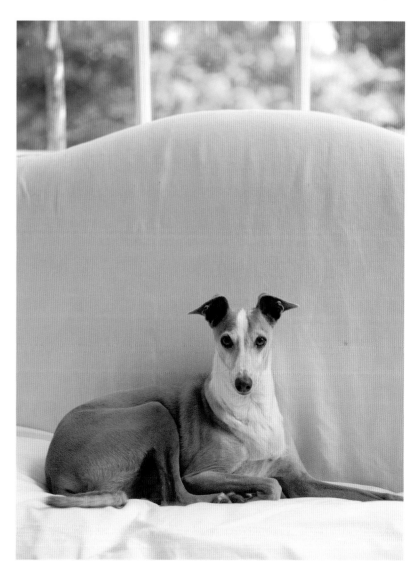

Furlow uses simple boards for the interior walls of all his houses. In the photograph above, top right, a blue plastic liner from the Dollar Store lines a beautiful silver goblet/ice bucket on a drinks tray in the Barn. On the preceding spread, the floor of the Lumpkin House center hall features Bob Christian's stunning paint effects.

ACKNOWLEDGMENTS

First and foremost, my heartfelt thanks go to Bunny Williams. Her tireless work and vision have made this book possible. Bunny insisted that my properties would be of interest to many people. My gratitude and appreciation go to John Rosselli, for just being John Rosselli. I am blessed by their friendship.

Then there is Julia Reed—she is something else! Julia is a gifted writer and an incredible cook. I knew we would be fast friends when she came into my home with three-inch-thick pork chops, with just as much fat as pork. She brought the pork chops from New Orleans. I still dream of them. She also brought her dog, Henry, and there was a mutual admiration between her dog and mine.

Now, for the photographer, Paul Costello, and his assistant, Alex Darsey. Paul and his wife Sara lived in New York for many years and now reside in the Garden District of New Orleans. My friend, Rodney Collins, an Americus native, lives in Atlanta during the week taking pictures of houses for his sister Glennis Beacham. Glennis is a leading realtor with Beacham and Company, and Rodney is a super photographer, who is always "ready to take a picture." He also encouraged me to complete this book.

I am grateful to Rizzoli publisher Charles Miers and editor Sandy Gilbert, for their enthusiastic embrace of this project as soon as John and Bunny introduced them to it. To Doug Turshen, the book's talented designer, who presented my "follies" in the most extraordinary way. And again to my wonderful editor, Sandy, who expertly pulled all the pieces together.

I am also grateful to Jimmy and Kay Fuller. Kay has a wonderful shop in Albany, Georgia. My gratitude and appreciation go to Larry Boyd, Tray Pierce, Manuel Avrilla, James Martinez, José Morales, and Patty Mock, Jimmy's secretary, who always seems to get the bills out on time. Thank you, Britt Miller, for building my two pigeon houses and all the gingerbread on the Peacock House. Big thanks to Joe McElroy for doing anything one asks. You are invaluable!

They don't come any better than Bob Christian and his assistant, Michael Carnahan, when it comes to faux painting. The two of them paint all over the country and are very much in demand. Bob's family has lived in Americus for four generations. They have always been known for their wit and good humor. Bob and his wife, Julia, also an artist, started out in New York City with John Rosselli. They now live in Savannah, Georgia, with three boys, who are artists as well. Bob's brother, Howard, also worked at John Rosselli and Treillage. Howard is now with *Architectural Digest*.

I would like to thank not only my friend Martha McLanahand for her support as well as the crowd at John Rosselli's and Treillage for putting up with me all of these years: Dennis Schaffer, Philip Sleep, Nicola Fiorelli, Haynes Wheeler, Mari Ann Maher, John Sneed, Dennis Ford, Jackson McCard, Phillip Formeloza, Rex Banada, Shelley Selip (John Rosselli D&D, NYC), Carolyn Coulter (Bunny William's assistant), Darcy Fulton, and last but not least Jonathan Gargiulo, John Rosselli's nephew, who keeps everything under control—except for John Rosselli's buying!

—*Furlow Gatewood*

I will never be able to thank Bunny Williams and John Rosselli enough for introducing me to their great friend Furlow Gatewood. Being granted entrance to Furlow's enchanting world is an incomparable gift. I have learned much from all three about how to live—not just stylishly (though that is certainly the case), but generously and joyously, surrounded by a beloved menagerie of animals and people. I also want to thank our editor, the marvelous Sandy Gilbert for her deft touch, her innate understanding of the subject matter, and her endless patience with me. All of us owe a huge debt to the designer, Doug Turshen, who did his usual stellar job of bringing the project to life on the page. Finally, Henry would like to thank Furlow's four canine companions for sharing their supper and making him feel so very much at home.

—*Julia Reed*

PHOTOGRAPHY CREDITS

RODNEY COLLINS: back of jacket, front endpaper opposite page 1, back endpaper opposite page 224, pages 2, 6, 11, 17, 19, 22, 26–27, 35, 36, 41, 42, 57, 64, 66, 67, 68–69, 71, 73, 74–75, 80, 98–99, 121, 132, 135, 142, 143, 144, 145, 148, 149 (top and bottom left), 150, 151, 154, 155, 166, 168–169, 170, 172, 174, 175, 176–177, 178–179, 180, 192, 193, 194 (bottom right), 195, 196, 197, 198, 200, 201, 202–203, 209, 211 (top left and right), 212, 213, 214, 215, 217, 220, 221, 222

PAUL COSTELLO: front of jacket, pages 5, 9, 21, 23, 24–25, 28–29, 30. 31, 32, 33, 34, 37, 38–39, 40, 43, 44–45, 46, 47, 48–49, 50, 51, 52–53, 54, 55, 56, 58–59, 60–61, 62, 63, 65, 76, 77, 78, 79, 81, 82–83, 84, 85, 86, 87, 88, 89, 90–91, 92–93, 94, 95, 96, 97, 101, 103, 104, 105, 106, 107, 108, 109, 110, 111, 112, 113, 114, 115, 116, 117, 118–119, 120, 122, 123, 124–125, 126, 127, 128, 129, 130, 131, 133, 137, 138–139, 140, 141, 146, 147, 149 (top and bottom right), 152, 153, 156–157, 158, 159, 160–161, 162, 163, 165, 171, 173, 181, 182, 183, 185, 186, 188, 189, 190, 191, 194 (top left and right, bottom left), 199, 205, 207, 208, 211 (bottom left and right), 216, 218, 219

Drawing on page 6 by Bob Christian.

Map endpapers by Jimmy Fuller.

First published in the United States of America in 2014
by Rizzoli International Publications, Inc.
300 Park Avenue South
New York, New York 10010
www.rizzoliusa.com

2015 2016 2017 / 10 9 8 7 6 5

Printed in China

ISBN 13: 978-0-8478-4252-0

Library of Congress Control Number: 2013953186
Project Editor: Sandra Gilbert
Art Direction: Doug Turshen with David Huang

LUMPKIN HOUSE

Pigeon House

PEACOCK ALLEY

PEACOCK LANE

Pigeon House

CUTHBERT HOUSE

ANDERSONVILLE Rd.